afterimage

by Robert Chafe
adapted from the short story by Michael Crummey

Playwrights Canada Press
Toronto

PLAYWRIGHTS CANADA PRESS
The Canadian Drama Publisher
215 Spadina Ave., Suite 230, Toronto, ON Canada M5T 2C7
phone 416.703.0013   fax 416.408.3402
orders@playwrightscanada.com • www.playwrightscanada.com

The publisher acknowledges the support of the Canadian taxpayers through
the Government of Canada Book Publishing Industry Development
Program, the Canada Council for the Arts, the Ontario Arts Council, and
the Ontario Media Development Corporation.

  ONTARIO ARTS COUNCIL
CONSEIL DES ARTS DE L'ONTARIO

Cover image of Melanie Caines by Justin Hall, courtesy of Artistic Fraud
Cover and type design by Blake Sproule

LIBRARY AND ARCHIVES CANADA CATALOGUING IN PUBLICATION

Chafe, Robert
Afterimage / by Robert Chafe ; adapted from the short
story by Michael Crummey.

A play.
Adaptation of a short story by Michael Crummey.
ISBN 978-0-88754-903-8

I. Title.

PS8555.H2655A77 2010   C812'.6   C2010-902066-9

First edition: April 2010
Printed and bound in Canada by Canadian Printco, Scarborough

For Michelle

Michael Crummey.

I expect that *Afterimage* would never have come into being if not for the fact that Jillian Keiley (founder of one of the country's most innovative and fearless theatre companies, Artistic Fraud) is terrified of flying.

Jill and I first met at the Labrador Creative Arts Festival in Happy Valley-Goose Bay in 1998. The week-long event invites professional artists in all disciplines to run workshops with school kids from across Labrador. The night before she flew back to St. John's, Jill was already stressed about the thought of getting on the plane. I gave her a copy of my second book, *Hard Light*, a collection of stories and poems about outport Newfoundland. This will keep your mind off it, I told her. I meant it as a joke, but Jill claims she read the whole way home and never gave a thought to the imminent crash that usually occupies her time during a flight.

A few months later she contacted me to suggest adapting parts of the book for the stage. Eventually *Salvage: The Story of a House* went up in an old merchant residence in St. John's, the audience moving from room to room in groups of eight to hear a series of three-minute monologues. Each small group carried a map that told them which room to move to next, a hundred people jigsawing through the narrow hallways, the actors on the move between pieces as well. Everyone saw the same show, but each in a different order.

I remember thinking, when Jill first described this Rubik's Cube of an idea to me, that there was no way to make the logistical nightmare work. I was wrong, of course. And as I've learned from that experience and my subsequent run-ins with Artistic Fraud, Jill's mind operates in a realm completely different than my own.

* * *

When Jill and Robert Chafe invited me out to lunch three or
four years ago, I was expecting the unexpected. Several times
after the *Salvage* show Jill had mentioned that she might be interested in adapting "Afterimage" for the stage. Fill your boots,
I told her, though privately I thought it was a ridiculous notion
and would never happen.

The story is part of *Flesh and Blood,* a collection set in a fic-
tional mining town that is remarkably similar to the place where
I was born and raised in central Newfoundland. I have only the
vaguest recollection of how the story came to me and how it
took shape, but there were a number of real-life anecdotes at
the root of it: a French woman who worked at the hospital in
Buchans and told fortunes in her off-hours; a family friend who
was badly injured in an industrial electrocution; ball lightning
entering an outport house through the stove and circling the
room until it was swept out the door with a broom. Why these
completely unrelated events began circling one another in my
head is a mystery to me. But they created a gravitational field
that pulled in dozens of other stray incidents and stories I'd
heard: the worm that curled up and died when held in the palm
of the seventh son of a seventh son; the kids of an ostracized
family who passed on a contaminating "touch" if you came into
contact with them; the travelling photographer who went door
to door in Buchans when I was no more than five or six years
old. The episodic nature of the source material made for a story
told in a series of brief scenes weaving back and forth across a
number of time frames, many of them offering variations on images of fire or electricity. Not the kind of thing that seems to be
crying out for a theatrical treatment.

Over lunch, Jill explained her plan to build an "electrified"
set with a copper floor and copper-wire walls with a live current
running through them. She wanted to wire the actors' costumes
in a way that would allow them to complete a circuit in order
to spark off one another or illuminate light bulbs by touch or
mimic the flash of a camera. She sketched a few things on nap-
kins, talking at length about the difference between AC and DC
currents. I knew enough about Jill by then not to dismiss the lu-
natic notion outright.

Robert, likewise, took it all in without batting an eye. He and Jill have been collaborating for years, and nothing she suggested seemed to give him the slightest pause. I've been following Robert's work since moving home to St. John's a decade ago, from his one-man show, *Charismatic Death Scenes,* to the brilliant bare-bones period piece, *Tempting Providence,* to what was his most recent work with Jill at the time, *Belly Up,* a risky meta-narrative about a blind man trapped in an apartment with a wall mirror that alternately reflects the room's interior and the blind man's thoughts. He was being charged with writing a script based on my story that incorporated an electrified stage and an as-yet-unwritten original score setting some of the show to music. He seemed perfectly calm about it all.

The central conflict in "Afterimage" revolves around an orphan trying to figure his place in a peculiar family, a child who feels excluded by his normalcy and takes extraordinary measures to fit in. Robert's plays, it seems to me, are always about people trying to make connections, about an individual's struggle to find their place in a world that on the surface might suggest they don't belong. And for all the choreography and stage wizardry Jill employs, story is central to her shows. The pyrotechnics are always meant to illuminate or act as a metaphor for the human drama at the heart of the piece. If there was a pair to make something of "Afterimage" on stage, I was sitting with them.

They spent a long time that afternoon talking about staying true to the spirit of the story and how they planned to translate that to the theatre, but they needn't have bothered. They had me at hello.

* * *

I was in Toronto for the premiere of *Afterimage* at the Harbourfront Centre in April of 2009. It was a surreal experience to watch the play unfold, to have a vague sense of connection to characters and lines and images in the play and at the same time to recognize that the story as it was presented belonged wholly to someone other than myself.

Robert invited my input and involvement at all stages of the adaptation, but with the exception of some general conversations I left it to him. The little story I'd published was already more than a decade old and I've long since forgotten what interested me enough to write it. Robert and Jill had found something of their own in it and the best I could do for them, and the play, was to get the hell out of the way. And though there's an undeniable family resemblance between the short story and the theatrical incarnation, they are completely different creatures, with their own personalities and idiosyncrasies. This current version of *Afterimage* has been workshopped and rewritten since its debut and in some ways has moved even further afield of what the original story was. Which makes it more true to itself.

At the Harbourfront after-party, I was offered congratulations by a steady stream of well-wishers. I felt like a father handing out cigars in the waiting room while the mother recovers from the shock and awe of labour somewhere in the bowels of the hospital. I may have unknowingly planted the seed, but everything that followed in the gestation and birth of the play—everything that really matters—is the work and heart and vision of Artistic Fraud, and of Robert and Jill in particular.

—Michael Crummey

Afterimage received its premiere production from Artistic Fraud of Newfoundland at the Enwave Theatre of the Harbourfront Centre in Toronto on April 16, 2009, as part of World Stage. The company was as follow:

Lise	Mary-Colin Chisholm
Winston	Christian Murray
Theresa	Melanie Brooks
Jerome	Kevin Woolridge
Leo	Colin Furlong
Maggie	Petrina Bromley
Leonard	Phil Churchill
Connie	Melanie Caines
Director	Jillian Keiley
Score and	
musical direction	Jonathan Monro
Set design	Shawn Kerwin
Costume design	Marie Sharpe
Lighting design	Renate Pohl
Technical director	Rick Banville
Production manager	Erin French
Stage manager	Flora Planchat
Assistant director	Anita Rochon
Assistant director	Michael Worthman

Afterimage was written with generous assistance from the Canada Council for the Arts. Artistic Fraud developed the piece with pre-production dramaturgy by Iris Turcott, and post-production dramaturgy by Sarah Stanley.

Characters

Lise	the mother of the Evans clan
Winston	the father
Theresa	the oldest
Jerome	the youngest
Leo	the middle child
Maggie	a nurse
Connie	a young woman
Leonard	a photographer

A Note on the Chorus

The chorus in this play is built from the eight characters listed above. While they seem to have moments of omnipotence, chorus lines dedicated to a particular character are unique to their perspective and emotional arc and should be approached as such. The goal is to create the sense of communal storytelling, both in first-person action and in third-person commentary.

A Note on Setting

Afterimage was written to be performed in an electrified environment. Artistic Fraud's production included a set made of copper, and costumes wired to transmit live DC current. While the voltage was kept low and every precaution was met to ensure the safety of all actors and staff, the living electricity component allowed for all effects listed in stage directions. Thus, where noted in the play, sparks, flashes, fire, and the like were manifested quite literally in production.

A Note on Production

Afterimage was accompanied by an original score for voice and guitar-string harp performed by the ensemble.

Lights up on WINSTON, *his back to us. He stands centre stage, looking up at a hydro pole. In his hand is a downed power line. A pause on this.*

CHORUS (WINSTON) It does strange things to people, to not be connected.

The others enter as they speak.

CHORUS (LISE) People need to feel that spark.

CHORUS (MAGGIE) In our town, people need hope, that's all. And when they need hope they need the priest.

CHORUS (LISE) Sssh.

She plucks a harp string.

You hear that?

MAGGIE *shakes her head no.*

CHORUS (WINSTON) What people need are men who can climb.

He takes the line and walks to the hydro pole, begins to climb through the following.

CHORUS (THERESA) People are afraid. That's all.

CHORUS (LEONARD) Afraid of the future.

CHORUS (LISE) The past.

CHORUS (JEROME) Red hair.

CHORUS (THERESA) They throw rocks.

CHORUS (JEROME) Call names.

CHORUS (CONNIE) Here, the doctors they always arrive late.

CHORUS (LISE) The nurses, they need to be brave.

CHORUS (MAGGIE) In our town…

CHORUS (LEONARD) Pictures can't help it, they tell the truth.

CHORUS (LEO) Even when you don't want it.

CHORUS (LISE) But the truth is worth telling.

CHORUS (CONNIE) Like how love can hit you hard, leave you
bleeding.

CHORUS (LEONARD) And promises are hard to keep, but secrets
even harder.

CHORUS (LEO) In our town, fire reveals everything.

> *Beat.*

CHORUS (LEONARD) The future is a burden.

CHORUS (LISE) But people want to know it.

CHORUS (CONNIE) And when they want to know it, they go see
Lise.

> *A public place now, LISE is face to face with CONNIE and
> LEONARD. She surprises herself with what she says.*

LISE Congratulations.

> CONNIE *and* LEONARD *look confused and guarded.*

LEONARD For what?

> LISE *smiles and suddenly reaches with both hands and touches* CONNIE's *stomach.*
>
> *Behind and above them,* WINSTON *has made the connection between the downed wire and the pole and he is brutally shocked, a shower of sparks, noise, the buzz of the current through the space. The harp strings now powerful and loud when plucked, music.*
>
> *An emergency.* WINSTON *falls slowly from his height.* MAGGIE *races to prep the hospital space.*
>
> *Everything settles.*
>
> WINSTON *is laid out,* MAGGIE *with him.* LISE *stands a short distance away, staring, entering and stopped dead in her tracks by the sight of him.*
>
> *She speaks and startles* MAGGIE.

LISE Doctor not here yet?

MAGGIE Jesus.

What are you doing up here?

LISE Fresh linen?

MAGGIE Just… just lay it over there.

> *Beat.*

LISE Who is he?

MAGGIE   Evans. Winston Evans from out Springdale way.

You know him?

LISE shakes her head.

Wouldn't recognize him if you did.

LISE   Bad?

MAGGIE   Most of his body burnt. You can smell it down the hall.
Put most of the crowd off their lunch.

LISE   But not you.

MAGGIE   Or you.

Beat.

Loves yourself a bit of misery, don't you.

Gets to telling people so much bad stuff, you've taken a liking
to seeing it for yourself.

LISE   I don't tell them the bad stuff.

MAGGIE   No?

LISE   Nothing anyone can do about it, so don't do much good
to pass it on.

What happened to him?

MAGGIE   Don't you know already?

LISE   It don't work like that. Tell me.

Beat.

Tell me.

MAGGIE   Jesus. The windstorm last night, it took down a line of poles up the shore. The boys doing their best to get the juice back out to the bight, taking most of the morning. This fella on his second shift. Just graduated from the trades program they got themselves down in Stephenville. Up the pole like a fish scared of heights. Too nervous, and too near the lines. Weren't paying attention. And…

LISE   Fire in the wire.

MAGGIE looks at her.

MAGGIE   Sixty thousand volts. It's a wonder he's alive at all.

I had to cut off what remained of the workboots when they brought him in. His… his big toes came away with them, like pieces of leather themselves.

Poor soul.

LISE touches him gently. Beat.

LISE   He'll be fine.

MAGGIE   What did you say?

What did you just say?

LISE   He'll be fine, this one.

MAGGIE regards her, angry.

MAGGIE   Not to be made light of, this.

LISE   I wasn't.

MAGGIE   The man needs hope and good prayer. Not party tricks.

LISE   I know what he needs.

MAGGIE I mean it, Lise. Leave him be.

> *MAGGIE stares hard at her. LISE eventually turns and exits.*
>
> *MAGGIE gives WINSTON one more look and leaves herself.*
>
> *The man, still and alone. Silence.*
>
> *LISE slowly re-enters, looks back to WINSTON, speaks quietly.*

LISE Just fine.

You wait and see.

* * *

> *LISE, elsewhere, being watched.*

CHORUS (LEONARD) Lise Lacoeur.

CHORUS (CONNIE) She's the devil they say.

CHORUS (MAGGIE) Never miss her, walking the street.

CHORUS (LEONARD) That hair.

CHORUS (MAGGIE) Like some weird bird. Should be caged herself.

LISE This town is cage enough. Eyes beyond the bars, always staring in.

CHORUS (CONNIE) She's the devil.

CHORUS (MAGGIE) Sold her soul, they say.

CHORUS (CONNIE) Black magic, they say.

> *LEONARD at LISE's door.*

CHORUS (LEONARD)   Except the magician hides the trick.

CHORUS (CONNIE)   If there's a trick to it, bully for you if you
can spot it.

> *LISE's home. She doesn't notice LEONARD standing in the open*
> *doorway behind her, watching.*

LEONARD   Lise Lacoeur.

> *She turns, stares at him.*

The door was open, so.

I didn't mean to startle you, I—

LISE   No, of course not. No.

> *He offers his hand.*

LEONARD   Butler. Leonard Butler.

> *They shake. An energy between them, Butler stares at her.*

I've come to take advantage of your services. I hope it's not a
bad time.

> *Silence. They stare at each other.*

Is there a problem?

LISE   No. It's just... not often I get a man seeking my help.

LEONARD   Call it a curiosity.

LISE   And how did you come to hear about me?

LEONARD   I dare say there's not a worm under a rock that haven't
heard tell of you. And of course we've met before.

LISE   Have we?

LEONARD   Last week. In town. I was with a young lady, you offered your opinion. For free, unsolicited.

LISE   Yes.

Yes, I recall. Please take a seat.

LEONARD   Powerful thing to witness, Mrs. Lacoeur.

LISE   Lise, please.

LEONARD   Fascinating, really. Found myself wondering, where would a person learn such a trade?

LISE   My mother had the sight, and her mother before her.

LEONARD   Passed on then, like your red hair. A blessing.

CHORUS (CONNIE)   A curse.

LEONARD   Heard tell of people who can read auras. Heal by the laying of hands.

Tell me, what's it like? What is it that you see?

LISE   Uh, time. Moving. The way a… a fire moves through a forest.

LEONARD   Uh huh. Pictures.

LISE   The negative of pictures, darkness and light reversed.

Time, just it's… it's turned inside out.

LEONARD   Also heard tell of a seventh son of a seventh son, they say a worm held in his palm would curl up and die in a matter of seconds. Like it was laying in a bowl of pure electrical energy.

LISE   Seen it myself.

LEONARD   Bullshit.

Beat.

You're full of bullshit.

LISE   Why are you here, Mr. Butler?

LEONARD   Curiosity, like I said.

LISE   I don't think I can help you.

LEONARD   That young woman, what you told her, us.

LISE   Unwelcome news?

LEONARD   No news. She's not pregnant.

LISE   Not yet.

Beat.

LEONARD   It was inappropriate. The implication.

LISE   There was no implication.

LEONARD   She happened to be with me, and in a pubic place.

Beat.

Look, I'm just taking her picture, she wanted her pictures taken. I'm a professional.

LISE   And you're married.

Aren't you?

Beat.

LEONARD Yes.

That comes with… responsibility. You know that, don't you?

CHORUS (WINSTON) Single.

CHORUS (CONNIE) Unlovable.

CHORUS (MAGGIE) Alone with her devilry.

LISE Yes. I can imagine.

LEONARD It would be horrible for anyone to get the wrong idea. Telling her she'll be pregnant. While she's with me. It would be horrible for her to get the wrong idea.

> *Beat.*

LISE Give me that.

LEONARD What?

LISE I need something of yours, personal.

> *She snatches his handkerchief from his lapel pocket, places it in a porcelain bowl, sprinkles it with lighter fluid.*

LEONARD I feel like you're not listening to me.

LISE You came for my bullshit, and you'll hear it.

LEONARD Nobody needs what you have to give.

LISE And still people will come.

CHORUS (CONNIE) Back door, cover of night.

LISE Some things people need to know.

LEONARD You like delivering bad news, Lise Lacoeur?

LISE   I don't tell people the bad stuff.

> *LISE lights the bowl, a brilliant fire and smoke. She stares into the ashes.*

CHORUS (CONNIE)   Laid out in front of you.

CHORUS (MAGGIE)   Like a Sunday suit, and with just as little shame.

CHORUS (CONNIE)   Tell you everything. Secrets deep as wells.

LISE   *(present tense)* Read the ashes.

CHORUS (MAGGIE)   The way you'd read the paper.

CHORUS (LEONARD)   A photo of the future, there in the thing itself.

CHORUS (CONNIE)   Blood in the body of a baby.

CHORUS (MAGGIE)   Blood.

CHORUS (CONNIE)   A child.

CHORUS (MAGGIE)   Blood and pain.

CHORUS (CONNIE)   Pain.

> *LISE recoils from the image.*

LEONARD   What. What!

LISE   You need to stay away from her.

LEONARD   Excuse me?

LISE   You need to stay away from her. You will only cause grief.

> *She sees more. Recoils.*

Oh Jesus. Jesus!

LEONARD   You're trying to scare me now?

LISE   Can you leave, please. I can't tell you anything more.

LEONARD   You can't or won't?

LISE   Please, Mr. Butler.

LEONARD   Finish what you started.

LISE   I can't tell you any more.

LEONARD   Listen, you bitch—

LISE   Leave, please.

LEONARD   I'll have you fucking strung up!

LISE   Leave! Now!

> *He considers pressing her further, decides against it. He goes to leave, stops in the door.*

LEONARD   If any of this get backs to my wife…

CHORUS (CONNIE)   Secrets. Deep as wells.

> *He leaves her.*

CHORUS (LISE)   Secrets.

CHORUS (CONNIE)   The future is a burden.

CHORUS (LEONARD)   She told nobody else what she had seen, for Leonard Butler.

CHORUS (LISE)   Nothing anyone can do about it. It don't do any good to pass it on.

CHORUS (LEONARD) The darkness of the ashes.

CHORUS (CONNIE) She told nobody of that.

CHORUS (WINSTON) Or of everything else she saw.

CHORUS (LISE) Winston Evans.

CHORUS (WINSTON) What she saw for this man. Burned and transformed.

CHORUS (MAGGIE) What she had said at the hospital, of her sight for his good recovery.

CHORUS (CONNIE) Fear.

CHORUS (WINSTON) That first time.

CHORUS (MAGGIE) Winston Evans.

CHORUS (WINSTON) She saw it all.

CHORUS (LISE) Just by touching him.

CHORUS (WINSTON) No burning scarves. No furrowed brow or sweat.

CHORUS (LISE) Just by touching him.

CHORUS (WINSTON) This man. This ruined body. The truth be told, it filled her with pity.

CHORUS (LISE) And so much more.

Desire.

CHORUS (WINSTON) Desire.

CHORUS (LISE) To lay beside him. To feel the ghost of the voltage still coursing through.

The hospital. LISE *stands watching him.*

WINSTON   Is there someone there?

LISE   You want a cigarette or something?

WINSTON   My grandmother was a smoker. Told me not to start, I'd only get hooked. Horrible feeling she said, to be dependant.

>   *Beat.*

You tell fortunes. That's what they say.

LISE   Do they?

WINSTON   You know they do.

>   LISE *smiles, prepares the washcloth and basin. Silence but for the occasional slosh of water.*

What do you see? Now.

LISE   A man who needs some sleep. I should finish and go.

WINSTON   Sleep when I'm dead. Sleep soon enough.

Tell me.

>   LISE *stops washing him. Beat.*

LISE   This is not my job, you know.

WINSTON   No?

>   LISE *shakes her head. A silence. Stares at him, the washcloth limp in her hands.*

I can't see you. What are you doing?

LISE Nothing.

She starts to wash him again.

WINSTON Feels good. Like you knows what you're doing.

LISE Well, I do work down in laundry.

WINSTON I look that bad, no one else was willing?

LISE I wanted to.

WINSTON Did you now?

LISE And you look fine. Better than fine.

WINSTON Take your word. But I'm suspecting you a liar.

LISE You're going to be okay.

WINSTON Yeah?

LISE You wanted to know what I see. That's it.

WINSTON That's what *they* tell me. Tell me something else.

LISE Something, like, what? What?

WINSTON Something, anything. They say you knows everything.

LISE All right. You… will leave here.

WINSTON One way or another.

LISE On your own two feet.

He smiles, unconvinced.

You wanted to hear it.

WINSTON   Sure. Tell me more.

LISE   You will marry.

> WINSTON *begins to laugh, hurting himself.* LISE *watches him blankly.*

WINSTON   Oh, shit. Hurts to laugh.

LISE   You shouldn't then.

WINSTON   Every time I move. Like it's ripping open, like it's—

LISE   Shhhh.

> *She washes him. Silence.*

WINSTON   Feels good.

> LISE *smiles.*

A fine groom I'd make. I can see the photos now.

> *Beat.*

Why did you want to do this? The smell. I can smell it myself. Stronger when they change the bandages. That don't bother you?

LISE   I don't know.

WINSTON   Why don't you stay down in laundry? The nice, clean sheets. Why you want to see this?

> LISE *suddenly but slowly bends and takes him into her mouth.*
>
> *A long silence, stillness.*
>
> *She eventually stands again. Looks at him unashamed.*

LISE It'll come back to you. Don't worry.

You want kids. You'll have them.

> *WINSTON is silent. LISE starts to get up, turn away.*

WINSTON How many?

If that's true, then tell me.

> *LISE thinks, sees it clearly for the first time. Behind her, in the distance, a flash of two children, a boy and a girl, red hair like their mother. It is so clear to her.*
>
> *And then suddenly something else, a sputtering light. Another child. An incomplete picture. Vague. And then gone.*
>
> *We are left with the image of two that slowly fades. LISE smiles with a tentative pleasure.*

LISE Two. A girl, and a boy.

> *She begins to collect her things.*

I'm back in tomorrow morning.

You hear me?

WINSTON I'm not going anywhere.

> *She goes to leave. He stops her.*

You said I'll have a wife.

What will she look like?

> *LISE smiles.*

LISE Like a witch. Red hair, green eyes. Left-handed as well as right. Born on Friday thirteenth.

WINSTON   Are you trying to frighten me off?

LISE smiles, a promise to return.

LISE   A boy and a girl.

She exits. WINSTON lays alone for a second. We can feel him smile.

* * *

The flash of photography.

THERESA (fourteen) and JEROME (twelve) stand still and silent centre, JEROME with his eyes closed. They share their mother's red hair, her freckles.

Darkness, another flash. We see LISE and WINSTON have joined the children, a nice family tableau.

CHORUS (LEONARD)   A fine picture indeed.

The tableau breaks. WINSTON is upset.

WINSTON   Jerome?

CHORUS (MAGGIE)   Mr. and Mrs. Winston Evans.

WINSTON   I'm speaking to you.

CHORUS (MAGGIE)   Cursed. Just like his wife.

WINSTON   What did they say?

JEROME   Nothing.

CHORUS (MAGGIE)   A cruelty it was, to pass it on.

WINSTON   They said nothing? That true, Theresa?

THERESA   Nothing new.

CHORUS (MAGGIE)   The children at school were like the rest of us. Looking at the Evans kids was looking at Lise and Winston.

WINSTON   Theresa, look at me.

CHORUS (MAGGIE)   Like looking at a dead animal.

WINSTON   You don't let people talk to you that way.

LISE   Winston.

WINSTON   No, they don't, Lise.

LISE   Just kids being kids.

JEROME   They were big, Dad, but not as big as you.

WINSTON   I'm going to talk to the principal.

LISE   Kids, Winston. All kids get teased, why should our own be any different?

JEROME   It was funny.

WINSTON   Well, I don't think it's funny.

CHORUS (MAGGIE)   Winston understood the cruelty of some children. He had been like it himself before the tables had turned.

WINSTON   Tell me what happened.

THERESA   Dad.

WINSTON   You can tell me, or the principal can.

> *Beat. The children stare at the floor. JEROME takes a breath and goes to speak, but THERESA gives him a jab and he stops.*

I'm waiting.

JEROME   And so were we, that's all.

> *THERESA sighs.*

WINSTON   You were told to come straight home.

THERESA   I know.

JEROME   And told to come home together.

THERESA   We were in the playground.

> *They start to tell the story. THERESA looks out.*

JEROME   What is it?

THERESA   A storm.

JEROME   Sun splitting the rocks.

THERESA   For now. But the wind is changing.

> *JEROME, eyes closed, looks up, smiles.*

JEROME   Looking through eyes closed. I can see you. One, two, three, four… seven birds on a wire.

THERESA   One for sorrow, two for joy. Three for a girl, four for a boy.

JEROME   And then a voice from behind us.

THERESA   Familiar.

JEROME   Mean.

WINSTON   Those boys.

THERESA   You know what my mother says about when you make a face like that and the wind changes?

JEROME   Supposed to stay like it forever.

THERESA   Too late. These two were always ugly.

WINSTON   They said that to you?

JEROME   *(looking back up)* Seven birds on a wire.

LISE   Winston.

WINSTON   Why on earth are kids so cruel?

THERESA   *(looks up where JEROME looks)* Seven for a secret that can never be told.

JEROME   All of us then, Theresa and me…

THERESA   And two boys big as bears.

JEROME   Looking up to seven birds on a wire.

THERESA   He's right, they said.

JEROME   And I was too.

THERESA   Seven. How does he do that?

JEROME   Squinting through his eyes, b'y.

THERESA   There's no magic here in these two.

JEROME   I wasn't squinting. But they wouldn't believe that.

THERESA   My mother says Lise Evans can tell you when you're gonna die.

JEROME   She doesn't tell people the bad stuff.

THERESA She says people with red hair, left-handed, they're all
 descendants of the devil.

JEROME I don't have no horns.

LISE Same as everything else, children. Fear turns you ugly.

THERESA Nothing to be scared of here, I said.

LISE Good for you.

THERESA Bang a rock and we'd still feel it.

JEROME So they did.

WINSTON They threw rocks?

JEROME Just one.

THERESA Good aim though.

> *She is hit.*

JEROME Theresa!

CHORUS (MAGGIE) Those children. Like all children.

JEROME Careful.

CHORUS (MAGGIE) Like everyone in town.

JEROME Careful not to touch 'em, they said.

THERESA It's okay. The rock didn't hurt.

CHORUS (MAGGIE) If a hand should brush an arm. Or even graze
 clothing.

THERESA Strong I am. Like my father.

JEROME   My dad could take your dad.

THERESA   That's what they said.

JEROME   If the sight of your dad didn't make him sick.

LISE   Jerome, enough.

JEROME   Winston Evans, the hamburger man.

LISE   Enough I said.

WINSTON   What else?

LISE   Winston.

WINSTON   What else?

> *Beat.*

Theresa?

THERESA   Evans family freak show.

Have people over for dinner, they charge admission.

> *There is a silence.*

WINSTON   This has an end. I'd like to hear it.

THERESA   It was my fault. I was stupid.

LISE   Don't say that, please.

JEROME   You weren't stupid.

THERESA   I should have known better.

JEROME   You just saw something.

She does. She moves to LISE.

CHORUS (MAGGIE)   All the kids. Everyone. Always.

THERESA gently touches her mother's cheek.

Careful not to come into contact.

Silence as she looks at her finger. She shows them.

THERESA   A lash. Make a wish.

JEROME   Just like that, it was.

WINSTON   Then?

JEROME   Then.

THERESA   Then a whisper snaking through.

JEROME   You got the Evans touch.

THERESA   You got the Evans touch.

WINSTON   What?

THERESA   Silent.

JEROME   And invisible.

WINSTON   What?

THERESA   The Evans touch.

> LISE *stands, unnoticed by the family, lost in her own memory, encounters with the town. Memories of her own spark of the Evans touch gets passed.*
>
> *Folding a sheet with* MAGGIE *at the hospital. They touch hands. Spark.*

CHORUS (MAGGIE) No way to rid yourself.

JEROME Got to pass it on.

WINSTON What's that?

THERESA Pass it on, they said.

WINSTON What is that?

> *Snatching LEONARD's handkerchief from his pocket. He recoils. Spark.*

CHORUS (LEONARD) Like a germ.

JEROME Spreads. Moving through the schoolyard.

THERESA Hand to hand.

JEROME It's special. You got to be an Evans to carry it.

> *Touching CONNIE's belly in the town square. She is shocked. Spark.*

CHORUS (CONNIE) A living thing itself.

CHORUS (MAGGIE) Indiscriminate.

CHORUS (LEONARD) A will of its own.

LISE Enough!

Enough.

Please.

> *WINSTON looks at her.*

WINSTON *(looking at LISE)* Are you hearing this? You got to be an Evans to carry it.

JEROME   Yeah.

THERESA   Any Evans at all.

JEROME   Except for Leo.

> LEO *has entered the room, standing with his red cap in his hand, looking at the family.* LISE *reaches out to him, touches his shoulder, and does not get a spark.*

WINSTON   I'm hearing the story here.

> LEO *shrugs.*

Your brother and sister were waiting for you.

THERESA   Dad.

WINSTON   Waiting for you and getting hit by rocks.

THERESA   I didn't say that, Leo.

CHORUS (CONNIE)   The middle child.

WINSTON   Leo?

CHORUS (CONNIE)   Quiet.

WINSTON   Leo, I'm talking to you.

LEO   Sorry.

CHORUS (CONNIE)   Withdrawn.

LEO   I'm sorry.

CHORUS (CONNIE)   Living on the fringe of the family, like a leper outside a city in the Bible.

LISE   Supper's getting cold. Back to the table, please.

WINSTON   Where were you?

THERESA   Leo came then, and they backed off. Like the gulls when the wind picks up.

He didn't even hear what they said.

LEO   Yes I did.

LISE   Please. Like a family. Come now.

JEROME   Why don't Leo carry it? The Evans touch.

LISE   Jerome, enough.

JEROME   I'm just saying.

LEO   I don't know.

THERESA   Because of your brown hair.

LEO   Shut up.

THERESA   Poor Leo, they said.

JEROME   The boys big as bears.

THERESA   Poor Leo, having to sit to supper with the likes of that.

LEO   Shut up!

THERESA   Well, that's what they said.

LISE   Enough, please. Sit and eat. Winston.

WINSTON   Listen to your mother.

The family begin to silently sit.

Silence. LEO *watches his siblings across the table. Picks up his fork.*

LISE   Dig in Theresa, Jerome. It won't chew itself.

CHORUS (CONNIE)   Brother and sister, they had their mother's red hair, freckles. Left-handed.

LEO spills food on himself.

LISE   Leo, eat properly, please.

LEO switches his fork back to his right hand.

I have a person coming after supper. I trust I can leave the dishes?

THERESA nods.

JEROME   Leo can't. He's playing ball.

LEO   I can do the dishes.

JEROME   He's playing ball with those boys.

LEO   Jerome, you weren't listening again. I can do the dishes.

WINSTON   You know those kids?

LEO shrugs.

THERESA   They just asked him to play.

LEO   I'm not going. I never have.

THERESA   It's because your hair is brown. That's all.

LISE   Hat off at the dinner table, please.

LEO doesn't take it off.

WINSTON   Leo, your mother asked you to take off your hat.

He removes his red hat.

LISE   Theresa, you didn't eat all of your supper.

THERESA   I'm not hungry.

WINSTON   You were made a meal, you should eat.

THERESA   I had a big lunch, and late.

LISE   You didn't eat lunch.

WINSTON   You should know better than to lie to your mother.

LISE   You gave the lunch I made for you to the birds.

WINSTON   You see.

THERESA   I wasn't feeling well. Change in the wind.

LISE   Eat.

JEROME   I had lunch, Mom.

LISE   I know, dear.

JEROME   I had a sandwich and an apple.

LISE   And a chocolate bar bought with a quarter found in the couch.

JEROME   You know everything.

WINSTON   Handy, that.

JEROME   What about Leo? What did he eat today?

LISE smiles, looks at LEO. He stares at his plate. She turns back to the table.

LISE   Enough for now. You'll wear me out.

JEROME   Mom—

WINSTON   Enough, your mother said.

Silence. They eat.

LEO awkwardly handles his fork in his left hand.

LISE   Leo, please. Eat properly.

JEROME   You're not left-handed.

LEO throws down his fork, exits.

WINSTON   Theresa, Jerome, go to your rooms.

THERESA   The dishes.

WINSTON   Go, I said.

They exit.

Long silence.

LISE   I should get ready. My seven o'clock will be here the once. Don't like to be kept waiting. Help me clear?

WINSTON   Sour as milk in the oven.

LISE   Stop your fretting. Nothing too useful in that.

WINSTON   The last six months he's been worse.

LISE   You remember fourteen. A rage at the world for giving breath.

WINSTON   Theresa was nothing like it.

LISE   What do you want me to say, he's a boy.

>   *Silence.*

Headache now to stun a horse.

WINSTON   That so?

LISE   What is it, what's wrong?

WINSTON   Nothing.

LISE   Should know better than to lie to me. Said so yourself.

WINSTON   True enough. Come here.

>   *She doesn't move. He moves to her, takes her hand, holds it.*

LISE   Winston, please, can we not—

WINSTON   You said you saw everything. When you touched me that first time.

LISE   Yes…

WINSTON   And ever since, just by looking.

The same with the kids.

>   *She smiles and avoids his gaze, shakes her head.*

You can't see him. You can't see anything about him. Can you?

Leo.

>   *Beat.*

Can you?

LISE   You're worse than the kids. Please, I'm exhausted.

* * *

CHORUS (LEONARD)   Time turning inside out. Darkness and
   light reversed.

CHORUS (CONNIE)   And darkness. Sometimes only darkness.

The middle child.

   LISE is looking for LEO.

LISE   Leo?

CHORUS (CONNIE)   Like standing in front of light. Shadow and
   shape and no definition.

LISE   *(to THERESA)* Where's your brother?

THERESA   I don't know.

LISE   Time for bed, Leo, okay? Come on out.

CHORUS (WINSTON)   She said she'd seen everything with that
   first touch. The same with the kids.

CHORUS (JEROME)   Fire against the dark.

CHORUS (THERESA)   Bright spots moving, dancing.

LISE   Everyone else is in bed, honey.

CHORUS (CONNIE)   Leo was an eclipse. Questions and blackness.

LISE   I know you're in here.

CHORUS (CONNIE)   He spent as much time alone in the house
   as he could.

LISE Leo?

> *LISE opens doors throughout the house, searching in vain for LEO.*

JEROME Close the door, it's too bright.

CHORUS (CONNIE) Crawling into cupboards.

JEROME I don't want to go to bed.

CHORUS (CONNIE) Cubbyhole in the basement.

LISE Brush your teeth, please, no arguments.

CHORUS (CONNIE) He sat in complete silence.

JEROME I want Dad to tell me a story.

CHORUS (CONNIE) Comforted by the darkness.

LISE Well go ask him. But he's tired be warned.

CHORUS (CONNIE) Sometimes they didn't notice him missing for hours.

LISE Theresa, no reading past ten I said, that's final.

THERESA Momma.

LISE And no sulking.

CHORUS (WINSTON) It was killing Lise, to try to love without insight.

LISE Theresa, bed, now. Did you hear me?

CHORUS (CONNIE) Leo knew if he tried hard enough he could someday disappear all together.

LISE   I'm turning out the light.

CHORUS (CONNIE)   The middle child. The blind spot.

LISE   Good night, Leo.

> *Silence.*

> *She takes one final look around and extinguishes the light.*

> *A moment of darkness, and then* CONNIE *illuminates a light and finds* LEO *hiding.*

CHORUS (CONNIE)   A game Leo never wanted to win, but always did. His father upstairs in bed, wide-eyed in the darkness, thinking of ways to pull his boy back into the light.

* * *

> LEONARD *at the door,* LISE *answers it.*

LEONARD   Winston Evans?

> LISE *is stunned by seeing the man again. He doesn't recognize her just yet, it's been years.*

I'm looking for a Winston Evans.

LISE   Yes. My husband.

LEONARD   I hope I'm expected. Your husband—

LISE   Yes. The photographer.

LEONARD   Butler. Leonard Butler.

LISE   Yes. I'm sorry. Come in, please.

LEONARD   If this is a bad time, we can reschedule.

LISE   No. No, it's fine. My husband wanted these taken, be a shame to disappoint him.

Beat.

LEONARD   Yes, well, I have several packages and offers available. But this, this you may have heard of. Colour photography. Every colour of the rainbow, just as you'd see it. I have a brochure here which details and lists—

LISE   I'm sorry. We're of limited means.

LEONARD   I'm sure, but don't dismiss it outright. I haven't told you the damage yet. Lovely house by the way.

LISE   Thank you.

LEONARD   Been here long?

LISE   Fifteen years. Moved in just after our wedding.

LEONARD   We had a bugger of a time finding a place when we moved back last summer. Hot market right now.

LISE   Yes, I hear that.

LEONARD   If you're ever looking to sell, my brother's in the business, could fetch you double, triple what you paid.

LISE   We're happy here.

LEONARD   No, of course. I'm just saying, should you change your mind.

LISE   *(calling out)* Winston.

LEONARD   Have I ever taken your photo, Mrs. Evans?

LISE   No.

LEONARD   Are you sure? I feel like we have met.

LISE   I don't believe so. Winston!

LEONARD   And two children, is it?

LISE   Three. Three children. Winston must have told you that.

LEONARD   Three kids.

LISE   Yes, he told you that.

LEONARD   Yes, so he did.

Awkward silence.

LISE   Winston!

LEONARD   Are you sure I've never taken your picture?

LISE   Quite sure.

LEONARD   Not even before? Not as young as I look, you know. Used to moonlight here before me and the wife hit St. John's.

LISE   Never had my picture taken proper, I can swear.

LEONARD   It's gonna drive me crazy, that.

The family begins to enter. LEONARD is shocked by the sight of them, WINSTON's burns, the general oddness and sullenness of the rest. He does his best to hide it.

LISE   Here we are.

LEONARD   Yes. Yessiree.

LISE   Mr. Butler, my husband, Winston.

LEONARD   Leonard, please.

WINSTON   Good day to you.

LISE   And this is Theresa, Jerome, and Leo. Smile, children.

They don't.

LEONARD   Well. Well well well, what a handsome family you've got, Mrs. Evans.

LISE smiles and nods.

A handsome family indeed. Makes my job easy, eh?

He laughs nervously. They simply watch him.

Silence.

Perhaps we could do somewhere with a bit more light? Bit more colourful, say. Something outside, the backyard?

LISE   Backyard is a state. Set to gardening and lost the will. Bit of a dog's breakfast.

WINSTON   Lise and I were thinking something simple, here in the living room.

LEONARD   Are you positive? What with your lovely red hair, Mrs. Evans, and that of the kids. I'm sure I can find an angle out back that would—

He stops, looks at her. Silence.

WINSTON   Is there something wrong, Mr. Butler?

LEONARD   Red hair.

LISE   Mr. Butler is convinced that we met before.

LEONARD   Lise.

LISE   I don't have memory of it, got to say.

LEONARD   Lise Evans.

WINSTON   Lacoeur, before she met me.

> *The name strikes* LEONARD. *He stares at her, knows that* LISE
> *herself remembers.*

LISE   Mr. Butler was thinking colour photography. They can do
such things now.

WINSTON   What's the cost on that?

> LEONARD *stares at her.*

Mr. Butler?

LEONARD   Minimal.

I'll tell you what. I'm a family man myself. Wife, two kids. I
will take some in colour, and if you don't like the results, so
be it. I'll take the hit.

LISE   That's very generous of you.

LEONARD   What can I say. I'm a good person.

LISE   Come on, children, Leo. Here on the couch.

> LEO *doesn't move.* LEONARD *steps towards him.*

LEONARD   That's a nice set of eyes on you, son. Gonna break
hearts some day.

> *He touches* LEO *on the shoulder and gets a zap.*

Friggin' carpet.

LISE   Come, Leo. Sit by your mother.

> *Through the following is tableau after tableau of* LEONARD *pulling* LEO *back and forth across his family, different poses for a photograph no one seems to want.*

CHORUS (CONNIE)   His mother. It was all her fault, he was sure of it.

Even his father had scars that set him apart. Leo had no evidence beyond intuition, but he was convinced that his father's appearance was somehow connected to his mother as well.

Brother, sister. Father and mother.

And Leo. A piece of jigsaw that simply didn't fit.

> *Finally settles on* LEO *sitting at a distance from his family, and looking none too happy about it.*

LEONARD   You wanna take that hat off, son?

> LEO *obliges.* LISE *quickly puts it back on his head.*

LISE   That's okay, Leo loves his hat.

LEONARD   Sure. Okay, everybody smile.

CHORUS (CONNIE)   Leo could find nothing to smile about.

> *Everyone else does.*

LEONARD   Smile and open your eyes.

WINSTON & LISE   Jerome.

> JEROME *opens his eyes.*

LEONARD   And hold it.

The flash goes off.

LISE Oh my.

JEROME I can see stars. Momma, I can see stars.

LEONARD That'll pass, son.

JEROME Stars when I close my eyes, Momma.

LEONARD And one more for luck.

Another flash of the camera that repeats, fractures, turns into lightning. Silence and then thunder.

Another clap of thunder and lightning and all lights go out.

* * *

In the darkness.

THERESA Momma.

LISE It's okay, honey. We're here.

JEROME Blackout! Blackout!

THERESA Mom.

LISE Take Jerome's hand, sweetie.

JEROME I got her, Momma. Watch the corner, Theresa.

WINSTON Where is Leo?

LISE Leo?

WINSTON Jerome, go find your brother.

LISE Leo?

LEO   I'm here.

THERESA   I told you it was a bad one.

LISE   Nothing to be afraid of, darling.

THERESA   My head hurts.

LISE   It will pass, you know it will.

WINSTON   Leo?

LEO   I'm here, I said.

JEROME   I got him, Dad.

LEO   Let go my hand.

WINSTON   Let Jerome help you, Leo.

LEO   I'm okay.

LISE   That came on fast.

THERESA   I told you it was a bad one.

LISE   I know you did, sweetie.

>   *LISE lights a candle.*

I was hoping you'd all sleep through it. That's why I sent you to bed so early.

WINSTON   Must have taken out the transformer down the coast. Whole town is out.

JEROME   I couldn't sleep anyway. I'm wide awake.

LISE   Well, you are now.

WINSTON   Come sit, Jerome, away from that window.

JEROME   Why?

WINSTON   'Cause I said so.

LISE   Listen to your father.

> *Thunder shakes the house.* THERESA *jumps.*

It's all right. Nothing to be afraid of.

JEROME   God, you're embarrassing.

WINSTON   Jerome.

LISE   It's all right. She just got a surprise, that's all.

JEROME   How can you be surprised and afraid of something when you know it's on its way?

WINSTON   Jerome.

JEROME   I'm just saying.

LISE   Sometimes knowing things makes it even scarier.

> *Thunder.*

THERESA   There's not even enough light to read by.

LISE   Won't kill us for one night.

JEROME   Tell us a story.

WINSTON   Yeah?

JEROME   Like you used to before you started at the mill. A ghost story.

WINSTON   A scary story, eh?

LISE   No, please. No ghost stories. The last time, Jerome, you were up half the night.

JEROME   I wasn't afraid.

LEO   No, it was the bed shaking, not you.

JEROME   Shut up.

LISE   Your brother is just teasing, Jerome.

LEO   *(a teasing mimic)* God, you're embarrassing.

WINSTON   Listen to you, brave man.

> *He tickles* LEO, *who giggles and smiles widely. A nice family moment except for* JEROME, *who sulks.*

When I was little, your age or younger, growing up in Eastport. In a house with my mom and dad and grandmother. One fall night there was a thunderstorm, just like this one, rolled in off the sea. It was dark back then. At night. Not like now. There were no electric lights to read by, ever. So when clouds that heavy dropped on ya, well sir, it was pure black.

> *He blows out the candle. The children giggle. A crack of thunder and they start.*

LISE   Winston.

WINSTON   That storm there shaking the town. Our house, each room lit up, a constant flash of lightning. All of us frozen around the wood stove, too scared to move anywhere else. Kerosene lamp on the table, the flame in it itself shaken by the thunder. It was that bad. Well, Nan, she got up to add a junk of wood to the fire. Moving across the room like in slow motion. The sputter of light. And when she opened the stove

Newf. dialect

door, well, the lightning. Blue fire. It came right through the chimney. Right into the house. Ball of blue fire, right into the room with us.

It does. WINSTON *becomes lost in the memory of it, disturbed by it.*

Circling the room. Like an animal stalking its prey. Hungry. Angry. Spitting at the walls.

THERESA   What happened?

WINSTON   The rumble overhead.

THERESA   Daddy?

WINSTON   The silence in the room.

THERESA   Daddy, what happened?

WINSTON   The silence, except for that hum, that dry hum. Sizzle. Burn. Burning.

LISE   Winston?

Beat.

Winston.

WINSTON   My grandmother, she…

A figure can be seen in the darkness, a broom in hand.

JEROME   What, Daddy, what?

WINSTON   She just…

The figure moves towards the ball of light and with the broom sweeps it away into fire and sparks. Darkness.

JEROME Daddy?

> *LISE relights a candle. WINSTON is surround by his family,*
> *listening intently. WINSTON is distant, still disturbed by the*
> *memory.*

She what, Daddy?

LISE Enough scary stories for one night, please.

JEROME I'm not scared.

WINSTON She swept it outside.

JEROME She swept it outside? The lightning?

WINSTON Yes. That she did.

JEROME With a regular old broom?

THERESA Were you scared?

LISE Of course he was, it's a powerful thing. That's why you're
to stay away from the windows when told.

> *Thunder, THERESA starts.*

> *LEO stares at the candle. Moves closer to it.*

Don't stare, Leo. You'll hurt your eyes.

LEO Wouldn't the broom just burn?

LISE Leo, get away from that candle!

> *The family look at her.*

You'll hurt your eyes, honey.

WINSTON It's okay, Leo. Give it to me.

Beat.

JEROME   It must have been bright. The ball of lightning.

WINSTON   That it was, bright. The afterimage of it, for a good
fifteen minutes after.

JEROME   What's an after…?

WINSTON   Afterimage.

JEROME   Yeah.

WINSTON   It's when your eyes, when you look at something…
well here, try it, this candle.

> *WINSTON hands JEROME the candle.*

LISE   Winston.

WINSTON   Stare at the candle here, and don't blink. Yeah?

LISE   I just asked Leo not to.

WINSTON   Just for a second.

JEROME   I don't see anything.

WINSTON   Keep staring. Okay.

And now look away and close your eyes.

> *They do.*

Well?

JEROME   I can see it, I can see it.

WINSTON   Theresa?

THERESA A black spot? Moving, dancing.

WINSTON That's it. Leo?

> *He goes to give the candle to* LEO. LISE *gets up and takes it.*

LISE Winston, I said no.

LEO I want to see it.

LISE Well I asked you not to.

WINSTON Just let him look.

LISE Time enough now anyway. Should be in bed.

WINSTON Lise—

LISE I said no.

> *Beat.*

Come on, back to bed, everyone.

> *The children groan.*

No sulking now, I mean it.

> *The children begrudgingly start to get up.* LEO *gets up, wanders into the darkness.*

Leo?

Leo, come give your mother a hug.

> LEO *slowly moves towards her, stops short, stares at her.*

Leo?

> *He bends forward and angrily blows out the candle.*

* * *

Darkness.

In the darkness the noise and sparks of the Evans touch.

read.

(X)

*Lights illuminate the family in movements of connection;
WINSTON kissing his wife, JEROME shoving THERESA, a ballet
of points of connection, each one lit by the spark of the Evans
touch. LEO stands in the middle of it all, untouched and unaf-
fected. CONNIE walks slowly towards him, unseen. Before she
reaches him, the family have formed a tableau, the same one
that was the final pose for the photograph. A photographic
flash and then LEO dark and silhouetted against the pale blue
afterimage of his family.*

*The lights restore to normal. LEO stands by himself now in
the Evans home. Blood on his face.*

THERESA enters, looks at him. She has a cloth in her hand.

THERESA   How's your eye?

LEO looks to her, startled, doesn't say anything for a moment.

LEO   Still works.

THERESA   Gonna blacken up. Gonna make you look tough.

Guess you are though, aren't you?

Silence.

That was a stupid thing to do. Stupid, so most wouldn't call
it brave. Or tough.

LEO   So I'm stupid.

THERESA   Take no fortune told to know you were gonna lose
that one. He was twice the size of you.

LEO I got my share in.

THERESA A real mean streak too. Runs in his family, Mom says. Nothing a bit of anger or upset on your part could contend with.

LEO Did you hear what he said about you? And Jerome.

THERESA I heard fine.

LEO I don't care about my eye. As long as there's a bruise on him somewhere.

THERESA Why? He didn't say anything about you.

Silence.

The man delivered the picture today.

LEO What?

THERESA indicates where it hangs. LEO slowly walks upstage.

CHORUS (LEONARD) The final product, framed and placed on a wall in the living room.

LEO stands beneath it, looking up at it.

In it, Leo's face, sullen, stoic.

CHORUS (CONNIE) The camera itself about to steal his soul.

THERESA Mom decided she liked the colours. Paid extra and didn't mind doing it.

CHORUS (CONNIE) Leo saw more than colour.

CHORUS (LEONARD) His family framed and contained.

CHORUS (CONNIE) Himself both within it and without.

THERESA Do you like it?

CHORUS (LEONARD) His family.

CHORUS (CONNIE) The first time he'd really ever seen it. A distance. Beyond red hair and freckles. A simple truth.

CHORUS (LEO) Confirmation.

THERESA Here, let me.

> *She moves to him and begins to wipe the blood. He stands back, still looking at the photo.*

LEO It doesn't make you mad? When they talk about you like that?

THERESA Jerome was laughing five minutes later. And if you want to know, the only bad memory I have of the day was my brother getting tossed like a leaf in the wind.

> *LEO brushes away her assistance. Walks away.*

You can't change things, Leo.

> *Silence.*

Leo?

CHORUS (CONNIE) To hear her say that.

THERESA What is it?

CHORUS (CONNIE) The futility in any attempt to alter himself or the world.

THERESA Leo?

> *He charges her.*

LEO   I could pull the copper-coloured hair from your fucking head.

He turns and runs off, leaving THERESA *speechless.*

* * *

LISE *and* WINSTON'*s bedroom. They enter mid-battle.*

WINSTON   He kicked a boy in the face today.

LISE   He just gave himself a good smack on the eye.

WINSTON   He didn't give himself anything.

LISE   If he's going to be picking fights…

WINSTON   Hiding for most of the day. When he does come out, face bunched like a fist.

LISE   Talk to your son, not to me. I've tried, I've—

WINSTON   Not you, not me, us.

LISE   Why don't we just call the cops. Lock him up.

WINSTON   This is not the boy we raised.

LISE   Don't you think that you are blowing this just a little out of—

WINSTON   Our son kicked a boy in the face, Lise!

It took two kids to tear him off. Our son got pummelled by kids two years older—

LISE   Winston.

WINSTON   Two years older than him, because he attacked them like a rabid dog.

Ignoring it isn't a solution.

LISE   You're the one full of solutions, not me, solutions and problems.

WINSTON   He can tell he doesn't belong.

LISE   That is a horrible thing to say.

WINSTON   That's how he feels.

LISE   You talking like that. He is a part of this family.

WINSTON   I'm not the one that needs telling.

LISE   You talking like that, you should be ashamed of—

WINSTON   This is not about me.

LISE   Enough.

WINSTON   Don't make this about me.

LISE   Enough!

Tell him when we need to.

WINSTON   When is that?

LISE   Not now.

WINSTON   He knows, Lise.

   Beat.

Whether we say anything or not, he knows.

   Silence.

LISE   It's just a phase. He'll get over it.

WINSTON   And you call yourself a fortune teller.

> *She looks at him.*

> *A long silence.*

LISE   You look tired.

> *She makes her way to sit beside him. Takes his hand.*

You do.

See it in your eyes.

WINSTON   They're putting me on nights again.

LISE   Don't they know that you have a family, a working wife?

WINSTON   They know well enough. They also know twenty-two men with more seniority. No choice.

LISE   You give in too easily, Winston. I see it in you time and time again. The way people talk to you.

> *He looks at her, looks away.*

> *Silence.*

We'll tell him. When the time is right, when he is ready.

I'll know when, I will.

> *Pause.*

I will.

I'm his mother.

* * *

The world divides and ends. A new one begins. Different, long ago.

The living room. LISE, *a candle now in her hand. She listens, sensing something.*

Is there someone there?

Silence. CONNIE *can be seen curled into one wall.*

Hello?

Silence. LISE *listens to it.*

Do I know you?

Silence.

This is my house. Do I know you?

CONNIE   You Lise Lacoeur?

LISE moves the candle, the light catches CONNIE. LISE *recognizes her instantly.*

Are you Lise Lacoeur?

LISE   I was.

CONNIE   You was?

LISE   Lise Evans now.

CONNIE   Oh.

Well then. Congratulations, good for you.

It's a nice house you got.

LISE   Thank you.

CONNIE   What I wouldn't give for a house like this.

Beat.

LISE   You must be cold.

CONNIE   I'm more than that.

LISE   Raining to drown a horse.

CONNIE   I met you. Last year. On the street. You remember?

LISE nods her head.

You see things.

You saw things.

A small pause, then LISE nods.

Load of bullshit. Always thought it a load of bullshit.

LISE   That why you're here?

CONNIE   I didn't believe a word of it.

A beat. CONNIE smiles, turns away from her.

Yes, indeed. I would love to have a house like this. A husband. You're a lucky woman.

Beat.

What's his name?

LISE   Winston.

CONNIE   He good to you?

LISE nods.

He give you kids?

LISE nods.

How many?

LISE   One. A little girl. Theresa.

CONNIE   A little girl.

CONNIE nods sadly.

LISE   A month old last Tuesday.

CONNIE stifles a sad laugh.

CONNIE   A lucky woman. That you are.

LISE   Who told you to come to me?

CONNIE looks at her.

CONNIE   I don't often do as I'm told. Gets me trouble, that.

LISE   I was right. Wasn't I?

CONNIE stares at her.

Silence.

How long?

CONNIE shrugs.

CONNIE   Don't matter. Do it?

LISE   Two months.

CONNIE looks at her. Nods.

Constance. That's you. They calls you Connie. Some people call you that.

Pause.

Why you here, Connie?

CONNIE Fortune. The word, the sound of it, you'd think it'd be about money, good news.

LISE What do you want to know?

CONNIE Your brand of bullshit is more useful than the doctor's, more useful to me now.

LISE You have questions about the father?

CONNIE No. No, my dear. I know the answers to those already.

LISE He left.

CONNIE Said he'd put me on billboards. Took my picture, and my soul with it.

Silence.

LISE You want some tea?

CONNIE I want to know about the baby.

I want you to tell me what will become of me and the baby.

A small pause.

Can you do that?

LISE You're upset. Maybe you should get some rest.

CONNIE They says you can do that.

Beat.

Please.

> *LISE looks at the ceiling, a tired and worried sigh. She thinks, CONNIE's eyes on her, pleading.*

> *LISE nods.*

LISE Yes. Yes, I can do that.

Give me your kerchief.

> *Silence. Then CONNIE smiles, disbelieving her own partici-pation in this, and gives LISE the kerchief. LISE prepares the bowl, CONNIE watching her every move.*

CONNIE You leave your door open like that, all the time? A body can just walk right in.

LISE You're not the first evening caller. Won't be the last.

CONNIE You knew how many months. You can see stuff like that. Just like that.

LISE Not showing yet, but the promise of it in the body. Intuition. The sight, true sight, that's something I got to work for.

CONNIE He must have the sight himself, natural. One look at me tonight and he knew himself a story.

LISE You got somewhere to go?

CONNIE I'll find one. Resourceful, me.

> *Silence as LISE continues with the preparations.*

Dreamer, see. That's half the problem. Think the best of peo-ple and the world. Trust the words that get said, trust them like gospel. Foolishness, it is. And stupidity. How many times a dog need to be get kicked before it gets shy of shoes? Me, I never learn.

Beat.

But that's it now. That's it. Whatever this is, be it boy or girl, this one, they should know better.

LISE   Boy or girl. You want to know?

CONNIE stares at her, then nods.

LISE sets the kerchief on fire. They both stare at it, a powerful and enforced quiet.

CONNIE   Just like that, is it?

LISE   A boy.

CONNIE smiles.

You got yourself a boy.

CONNIE   Just like that it is.

A boy. Well.

LISE looks back down into the bowl, her expression sliding, she stares slack-jawed.

She is unsurprised, deeply saddened, and disturbed.

Silence.

What?

What?

LISE   Nothing.

CONNIE   Nothing?

LISE   Nothing, it's nothing.

> *LISE has allowed herself to become upset. She gets up to walk away.*

CONNIE   That don't look like nothing.

Oh Jesus.

Oh Jesus, Jesus.

LISE   It's all right, I'm sorry. I shouldn't have, I shouldn't have done this for you. I should have sent you on your way.

CONNIE   Tell me what you saw.

LISE   It's going to be all right.

CONNIE   Don't lie to me. Tell me what you saw.

Please.

Please.

> *Beat.*

LISE   I can't.

CONNIE   You can't. Why can't—

LISE   I can't tell you. There's... there's nothing you can do about it.

CONNIE   It's bad.

> *LISE looks up at her. Silence.*

How do you know?

LISE I—

CONNIE How do you know there's nothing to be done?

> *LISE shakes her head.*

Send me out of here, not an ounce of hope. You can't be that cruel.

LISE I'm sorry.

CONNIE Tell me what to do.

Tell me how to save him.

> *LISE looks at her.*

You can do that.

> *She takes LISE's hand.*

You can do that.

> *LISE thinks hard for a second. She nods.*

> *She closes her eyes and grips CONNIE's hands tight.*

LISE It's…

It's going to hurt. The pain will be…

> *She opens her eyes and looks at CONNIE, who hangs on her words.*

Unnatural.

> *A beat and then lighting shift. CONNIE begins to cry in pain, doubling over.*

CONNIE Ah, Jesus Mary!

MAGGIE enters in a rush.

MAGGIE *(to LISE)* Glad you're here. Didn't know anyone else was on today.

LISE is silent, staring at CONNIE.

CONNIE Oh God! God!

CHORUS (LISE) Your stomach will be bursting.

CONNIE God!

CHORUS (LISE) A hot knife at your spine.

MAGGIE *(to CONNIE)* You picked a day, my dear. Some snow out there. Not fit for a dog. Didn't even call for it.

CONNIE's eyes roll up in her head.

Stay with me, honey. Doctor will be here the once.

My God, her hands are frozen.

CHORUS (LISE) The weather will be against you.

MAGGIE *(to CONNIE)* She walked in with no coat. Lise, get some blankets.

LISE doesn't move, stares at CONNIE.

CONNIE Help me! Oh Jesus.

MAGGIE Lise!

LISE finally moves to fetch some blankets.

We're gonna warm you up now. But you gotta calm down for me, okay?

CONNIE Oh God!

MAGGIE You gonna have to try to be calm. I'm not kidding around, okay? Lise, go call him again.

CHORUS (LISE) The doctor will be late. But you have to hold on.

CONNIE *(to LISE)* I'm trying, I'm trying.

MAGGIE You hear me, Lise? Get out and call him again. Tell him there are complications. Tell him to get here as soon as he can.

CONNIE Help me!

MAGGIE Lise! Go!

CHORUS (LISE) The minutes will stretch and the wind will howl inside you, and he will feel very angry, very angry at you, desperate to get out. But you have to wait. You have to wait for the doctor. You want hope, then that's it, that's all I have to give. That's all. You have to... try.

CONNIE Help me!

> LISE, *hiding outside the door, sings something to herself, breathy and panicked.*
>
> *She finishes singing, leaving a prolonged and eerie silence.* CONNIE *slowly comes around the door and looks down at her.*

CHORUS (CONNIE) You were right.

There's nothing anyone can do about it.

> *Beat.*

Don't leave him alone.

All right?

She vanishes.

LISE enters the room, CONNIE'*s body covered,* MAGGIE *watching her silently.*

MAGGIE   Bloody sin, it is.

LISE   Yes.

MAGGIE   Doctor called. Finally. Out to his cabin when the snow set in. Couldn't even get out to the shore road, let alone into town.

LISE   Unavoidable then.

MAGGIE   She was fine. She was a healthy girl. Young, strong. No good reason why this couldn't have been a better story.

LISE   Unavoidable.

MAGGIE   No good reason.

Silence.

Never tended a birth like that, not by myself, one like that. Didn't look natural, it didn't.

Stupid. I'm no doctor, don't even know, can't even say what it is that I did wrong.

LISE   Nothing.

MAGGIE   Don't even know what to write in the fucking report. I don't even—

LISE   Unavoidable.

You hear me?

The women stare at each other hard for a moment. MAGGIE *seems to understand the depth of* LISE's *sight for the first time and accepts her diagnosis, nods.*

Silence.

MAGGIE Bloody sin. It is.

LISE That it is.

MAGGIE She had his name picked out and everything. Convinced it would be a boy.

LISE Is he all right?

MAGGIE He's just about perfect, I'd say. Except for that little birthmark on his head there. Shape of a candle flame. But that's nothing. That should fade away soon enough.

LISE Will it?

MAGGIE I would guess.

> LISE *looks down at the boy. A heaviness in her that she fights to contain.*

You tell me.

LISE I can't.

> *She looks away from the boy, makes a big decision, shakes her head.*

Can't... can't tell you a thing about this one. Couldn't if I tried.

> *Silence.* MAGGIE *tries to smile, goes to exit.*

What was she going to call him? What's his name?

MAGGIE Leo. After his father, she said.

LISE Sounds about right.

> *MAGGIE exits. LISE looks down at the child, unsure of what to say or do.*
>
> *The baby begins to cry and LISE can't take it. She goes to leave, but when she gets to the door her milk lets go, the front of her uniform soaked. She pauses for a second, unsure of what to do, and then sorrowfully and against her own judgment goes back and picks him up carefully. She begins to breastfeed him, singing softly under her breath.*
>
> *Outside of time and place, all the others enter, stand behind her, watch her. WINSTON comes up behind her, puts his arm around her.*

WINSTON We can take him.

> *He takes the baby from LISE's arms and exits with the others.*

* * *

> *Back in the present, LISE stands back on, looking at the family photo. A long pause on this.*
>
> *The house is silent.*
>
> *THERESA enters quietly, sees her.*

THERESA Mom?

> *LISE turns to her, startled, gives her a smile, walks away from the picture.*

It's late.

LISE I know.

What are you doing up?

THERESA Couldn't sleep. Headache. Rain, maybe.

LISE Hmmm.

THERESA Where's Daddy?

LISE Working. He's at work.

How's your brother?

THERESA thinks, shrugs.

THERESA Jerome is snoring.

LISE I was talking about Leo.

THERESA I know.

Silence.

I was gonna do some reading.

LISE For a little while, okay? You should get some sleep when you can.

Silence.

You all seem younger to me, you know.

I know you're growing up. Young men and women. But there's no magic switch to make it so for me. In my heart and head.

All these secrets you have now. That's a very adult thing.

Beat.

THERESA I'm going to get a drink of water. You want some?

LISE   No. Thank you.

>   *THERESA goes to exit and stops.*

THERESA   He swore yesterday. Leo.

LISE   What?

THERESA   He said the F-word, when he was angry at me.

LISE   Why was he angry at you?

THERESA   I don't know.

LISE   No?

>   *Beat.*

THERESA   Because of my hair.

He didn't like the picture. I don't think so.

>   *Silence.*

LISE   Thank you for telling me.

THERESA   He'll be mad at me if he knows I did.

LISE   Thank you for telling me, Theresa.

>   *THERESA exits.*

>   *LISE looks back to the photo. Silence.*

>   *She turns back to the room.*

Leo?

>   *Silence.*

Leo, are you here, can you hear me?

Long silence.

Is your life so terrible?

Silence. LISE *looks mournfully at the ceiling, makes a decision.*

Leo. You should know.

CHORUS (CONNIE) In a quiet house without the creak or crack to guide her, and no fortune told to mark her success, Lise walked room to room, talking to her son. Telling him a story she now knew she should have told him before.

LISE Her name was Connie.

CHORUS (CONNIE) The tale and its truth spun like a fortune in reverse, repeated and more detailed with each room she walked. Every room in the house. Every room but one.

> LISE *enters her bedroom and begins to undress. Eventually stands in her bra and underwear.*
>
> WINSTON, *as chorus, slowly enters, unseen by* LISE, *and illuminates a dark place. There, we see* LEO *hiding, eyes glued to his mother.*
>
> *In the soft light, he comes close to* LEO *and speaks gently and slowly.*

CHORUS (WINSTON) From where he sat hiding in her closet, Leo watched his mother. He could see the constellation of beauty marks across her shoulders. The faint line of her ribs when she breathed.

CHORUS (LEO) Wanted to turn away, shut his eyes, shout something.

> LEO *keeps staring.*

LISE unhooks her bra, lets it fall to the floor. LEO still watches.

Silence as LISE brushes her hair.

CHORUS (WINSTON)   Leo couldn't recall ever having seen his mother like this. But he had a vague memory of her nursing him. The smell of her skin, her face leaning above him.

CHORUS (LEO)   Her voice saying his name.

LISE begins to softly hum the song she had sung earlier in the laundry room. A pause as LEO listens and watches her.

CHORUS (WINSTON)   He didn't understand why there was no visible sign to mark him as hers.

CHORUS (LEO)   Why he alone had been passed over.

CHORUS (WINSTON)   He thought of the warmth of her milk in his mouth. And then he felt it. A surge of loneliness, a great surge that emptied him like an overturned bottle.

LEO dashes from his hiding place, moving with a purpose past his mother towards the door. LISE, shocked and startled by him, covers herself.

LISE   Leo!

She struggles with her clothing as he runs out.

Leo! Wait, wait.

CHORUS (WINSTON)   He knew he should have waited until she was asleep, but—

CHORUS (CONNIE)   Something moving his arms and legs now.

CHORUS (WINSTON)   Something not connected to rational thought.

In the living room now, LEO grabs his mother's porcelain bowl. LISE still struggling to dress stumbles out of her room.

LISE   Leo, please, honey.

CHORUS (WINSTON)   Sorrow.

CHORUS (LEONARD)   Desperation.

CHORUS (WINSTON)   Anger.

He reaches up and takes down the family picture.

CHORUS (CONNIE)   Fury.

LISE   Come back, Leo.

CHORUS (WINSTON)   A long time in the making.

CHORUS (CONNIE)   A dark flower coming to bloom.

LEO sets the bowl and picture on the table. LISE begins making her way down the stairs, still putting on her shirt.

LISE   Come back up here, come on now.

CHORUS (JEROME)   Theresa and Jerome.

CHORUS (THERESA)   They had been marked by their mother.

CHORUS (WINSTON)   Left-handed.

CHORUS (THERESA)   Red hair.

CHORUS (CONNIE)   But this boy.

Retrieves a canister of lighter fluid. LISE is still making her way, her impatience growing.

LISE   I know you can hear me.

CHORUS (CONNIE)   This boy.

CHORUS (JEROME)   Not even left-handed.

CHORUS (THERESA)   Brown hair.

CHORUS (LEONARD)   Those eyes.

CHORUS (CONNIE)   Handsome.

> *He soaks the picture in the bowl.* LISE *nears the living room, furious now.*

LISE   Leo, I'm talking to you! Leo!

CHORUS (WINSTON)   The leper.

CHORUS (CONNIE)   The middle child.

> LEO *suspends a lit match above the bowl for the briefest of seconds.* LISE *enters the living room and sees him.*

LISE   Leo!

> *He drops it. A massive flash and noise.*

> *And darkness.*

* * *

> *At the hospital,* MAGGIE *races to* LEO'S *aid,* WINSTON *and* LISE *hover in a fit of worry.* MAGGIE *pushes them outside.*

> *They sit, tired, apart.*

> *A lengthy silence.*

What time is it?

> WINSTON *shakes his head.*

Silence.

WINSTON They'll give him something.

For the pain.

Pause.

Watch him. In case of infection.

Beat.

LISE He's gonna be okay.

He looks up at her.

Yes.

I believe that. He will.

WINSTON looks away.

WINSTON I was at work. Coming up on three in the morning. Raking through the flotation tank. My reflection down below, moving. And it was like it leapt up and washed over me. The sight of it. Oh God, passing through me, through my body just like—

LISE You saw.

WINSTON I could hear him, and when I closed my eyes I could still see it. I could still see the fire moving against the dark.

Beat.

That's why I was home.

LISE Before the ambulance.

Beat.

He's gonna be fine. He is.

WINSTON Yeah? You believe that?

LISE I know that.

WINSTON No. You don't.

LISE He's going to be fine.

WINSTON You said that about me.

LISE Yes and—

WINSTON And look at me!

Pause.

Will he be able to see?

Beat.

Tell me that. Will he be able to see?

The force of it threw him back against the wall. His little red hat gone, dust. Hair, gone.

LISE Winston—

WINSTON His forehead, cheeks. His face fucking cooked. His eyelids welded.

LISE Please, don't.

WINSTON They don't know about his eyes, they don't know that yet.

So, will he?

Beat.

Will he be able to see?

LISE   I don't know.

WINSTON   No you don't.

LISE   Please don't be angry with me, I can't take it.

WINSTON   It's just a phase. He'll get over it.

LISE   This is not my fault.

WINSTON   That's your guilt talking.

LISE   Please don't say this is my fault.

WINSTON   Jerome going to stub a toe, you buy him steel-toe shoes.

LISE   That's not fair.

WINSTON   No it's not, but it's true. You've never cared enough.

LISE   No, no, that's not true.

WINSTON   You've never been able to see for him.

LISE   I've only ever seen for him!

Beat.

This was all I could see.

I couldn't see anything else about him but this.

Beat.

Ever since I met his mother. Ever since that he's been blood and pain, I look at him and see ash and tears and I couldn't stop it. I tried so hard, but I couldn't stop it.

Beat.

I couldn't stop it. So I stopped. I stopped…

Pause.

WINSTON   You're his mother.

Beat.

LISE can't look at him.

Sometimes knowing things is scary. You've said that.

You say that.

Long, long pause.

He'll be in for at least three weeks. And out of it for a couple of days. You should go home.

They stand at separate ends of the room, unable to look at each other.

LISE looks up, making a realization, a sad smile.

LISE   Hmmm, this room. This is where I first saw him. Where I first saw you.

WINSTON smiles too, nods sadly.

LISE and WINSTON stand at LEO's bedside.

CHORUS (THERESA)   She didn't go home. Neither did he. He was consumed with fear for his son. The memory of that first time he saw his own face. The shock beyond anything that he could be prepared for. And he was a grown man.

CHORUS (CONNIE)   But Leo.

WINSTON Leo.

CHORUS (CONNIE) So young. Already so sullen. Already so sad.

CHORUS (THERESA) Three weeks at his bedside. Leo never spoke.

MAGGIE enters.

MAGGIE Good day, Winston. Lise.

LISE & WINSTON Good day.

LISE Maggie.

MAGGIE Good day, Leo.

MAGGIE lights a candle.

CHORUS (CONNIE) Her hands had tended to father, mother, and now tended to son.

MAGGIE Today is the big day, treasure.

We're going to remove these nasty old bandages for good. Sound all right?

Now I want you to remain really still, okay?

LISE Will it hurt?

WINSTON No.

MAGGIE Burns this deep, most nerve endings at the surface are destroyed. He won't feel a thing.

Hear that, Leo? Won't hurt a bit. But I do need you to remain still and patient. Winston, could you turn off the lights please?

MAGGIE *lights a candle and begins to remove the bandages.*

CHORUS (CONNIE)   Lise and Winston watched the process like the defusing of a bomb. Each step delicate and tedious. And one step closer to a frightening unknown.

She finishes. All look at the boy's face.

And when they saw their son again, neither could speak for the sight of it. Winston consumed with an eerie recollection. Lise studying the scars as though they were a map of his future.

MAGGIE   Don't open your eyes right away now, treasure. Take your time.

CHORUS (CONNIE)   The sadness and shock of it, and the boy's eyes were the only ones wet.

A pause and then LEO's *eyes slowly flutter open.*

Silence.

He stares blankly, seeing nothing.

LISE *suddenly takes the candle from* WINSTON, *brings it in front of* LEO. *He winces and shuts his eyes tight.*

WINSTON   Leo?

Leo?

LEO *eventually smiles.*

What is it?

LEO   I can see it.

CHORUS (CONNIE)   His eyes shut tight.

LEO I can see it.

* * *

CHORUS (LEONARD) He still hadn't said anything substantial by
the time they brought him home.

CHORUS (CONNIE) Taking his old quiet time, in brand-new
places.

> LEO *stands facing out, looking at something.* LEONARD *and*
> CONNIE *there with him.* LISE *looks for him around the house.*

LISE Leo?

CHORUS (LEONARD) The house itself still a state.

CHORUS (CONNIE) Burned and transformed.

LISE *(to THERESA)* Have you seen you're brother?

> THERESA *shakes her head.*

CHORUS (CONNIE) Ceiling full of smoke.

LISE Leo?

CHORUS (LEONARD) Broken bowl full of ashes.

CHORUS (CONNIE) Reminders, all.

> *She looks at* LEONARD *and they share a stare.*

CHORUS (LEONARD) Mistakes made.

> LEONARD *takes* CONNIE's *photo. She smiles and walks away*
> *from him.*

LISE Leo, honey, time for supper.

CHORUS (THERESA)   Leo abandoned his old habit of hiding in the house.

CHORUS (JEROME)   In favour of something else.

LISE   *(to WINSTON)* Have you seen Leo?

WINSTON   Not since this morning. Leo?

CHORUS (THERESA)   Looking in the mirror, studying the scars on his face.

CHORUS (JEROME)   Fluff of hair growing back in.

CHORUS (THERESA)   His lashless lids.

LISE   Leo?

LEO   I'm here.

> *LISE and WINSTON enter and stand behind him.*

WINSTON   Leo?

CHORUS (THERESA)   Everyone had been afraid for him.

WINSTON   Did you hear us calling?

CHORUS (JEROME)   Thought it be better for him not to regain sight at all.

WINSTON   Leo?

CHORUS (THERESA)   That he would never adjust to the change in himself.

CHORUS (JEROME)   But that wasn't what they saw in Leo now.

> *LISE walks to LEO.*

LISE   Hello, beautiful.

> *THERESA and JEROME enter the room as well, approach the mirror.*

CHORUS (THERESA)   There was a look of wonder in his eyes.

CHORUS (JEROME)   And something more than that.

> *LISE touches LEO's face, and for the first time it sparks with the Evans touch. LISE suddenly sees something, good and hopeful, so clearly it shocks her. She looks to WINSTON and smiles.*

CHORUS (THERESA)   Something.

> *The family all crowd around the mirror, seeing what LEO sees. Finally, the complete family tableau.*

LEO   Confirmation.

> *A flash of photography and lights out.*

> *The full family glowing in the blue-green afterimage, and then darkness.*

> *The end.*

photo by W. Evan Butler

Robert Chafe was born in St. John's, Newfoundland, where he currently works as artistic associate and playwright for Artistic Fraud. He is the author of numerous plays, of which *Butler's Marsh* and *Tempting Providence* were shortlisted in 2004 for the Governor General's Literary Award for Drama. Chafe has been a guest instructor at the Memorial University of Newfoundland, Sir Wilfred Grenfell College, and at the National Theatre School of Canada.